Caryn would like to thank Ken Lassman for showing her how to see and navigate wild weather in and beyond the Midwest for decades.

Both Stephen and Caryn thank Kelly Barth for her proofreading, and all our Indiegogo supporters, who made this project possible: Christina Gilbert, Julanne Patrick, Cheryl Unruh, Daniel McGauley, Helen Linda, Karen Faraca, Holmes Semken, Sandra Strand, James Skivers, Ray Liggett, Edwin Long, Elizabeth Millard, Juliana Zee, Suzi Reno, Irma Hudson, Anne Russ, Erin Sim, Lelain Lorenzen, Shari Dobbins, Christine Conner, Scott Mallin, Joy Lominska, Joan Vibert, Alta Bradford, Debbie Smith, Rachel Ellyn, Marty Stemmerman, Chloe Wagner, Ryan Hitchcock, Lori Dietrich, Susan Elkins, Mary Brandenburg, Sacie Lambertson, Denise Low, Brenda Beckner, Kelley Hunt, Al Berman, Jill Green, Elizabeth Merz, Kelly Speight, Craig Hagen, Jenny Brown, Edwin Long, Duane Daugherty, Ethan Hirsh, JoEl Vogt, Cathy Thomas, Kenneth Locke, Jane A. Vogel, Claudia True, Jenny Clark, Jana Svoboda, Lynda Vance, Elizabeth Wiltgen, Kat Greene, Sonja Swift, Arne Wilkin, Carol McGuire, Pauline Willison, Michael L. Bradley, Sandy Snook, Emily Sandelin, Olive Sullivan, Howard Roske, Ann Mayberry, Donna Fleetwood, Lynn Byczynski, Barry Goldberg, Noel Rasor, Lauren Pacheco, Morgan McCune, Cathy Callen Molineux, Brian Hagen, Kathleen Connally, Karen Roberts, Jaime Diaz, Katt Lissard, Linda White, Irina Souiki, Roy J. Beckemeyer, Maia Burnard, Lou Eisenbrandt, Debbie Hughs, Nancy Hubble, Thomas Kellogg, Judy Roitman, Maril Crabtree, and all our anonymous contributors.

Chasing Weather

Tornadoes, Tempests, Thunderous Skies in Word and Image

Caryn Mirriam-Goldberg & Stephen Locke

Ice Cube Press (Est. 1993) North Liberty, Iowa

Chasing Weather: Tornadoes, Tempests, and Thunderous Skies in Word and Image

Copyright © 2014 Caryn Mirriam-Goldberg and Stephen Locke

ISBN 9781888160826

Library of Congress Control Number: 2014934052

Ice Cube Press, LLC (Est.1993)
205 North Front Street
North Liberty, Iowa 52317-9302
www.icecubepress.com
e: steve@icecubepress.com
twitter: @icecubepress

Manufactured in the USA using acid-free, recycled paper. The paper used in this publication meets the minimum requirements of the American National Standard for Information Sciences—Permanence of Paper for Printed Library Materials, ANSI Z39.48-1992

Earlier versions of these poems appeared in:
❧ "Let the Rivers Clap Their Hands," "The Door of the Grass," "Beginner," "When the Rain Comes," "Field Love," "Coordinates," "Questions for Home," "Your Heart Has No Gate," "Imagine You Know How to Fly," "What the Field Says" and "Light" originally published in *Landed* by Caryn Mirriam-Goldberg. Lawrence, KS: Mammoth Publications, 2009 ❧ "Let the Rivers Clap Their Hands" and "The Door of the Grass" published in Little Balkans Review. ❧ "What Do You Believe In?" and "What Would Happen if You Walked Here?" originally published in *Animals in the House* by Caryn Mirriam-Goldberg. Topeka, KS: Woodley Press, 2004. ❧ "Questions for Home" published in *Connotations*. ❧ "The Light In Between" published in *I-70 Review*. ❧ "Welcome" and "Panorama" published in *Convergence*, edited by Marianela Medrano. ❧ "Finding the Moon," "Convergence," "After the Storm, the Stars" and "Enraptured" published in *Futures Trading*. ❧ "Supercell" published in *Storm Country*, edited by Claudia Mundell ❧ "When February Comes" originally published in the *Kansas City Star*.

Ice Cube Press Assisting Editor: Jennifer Moy

Table of Contents:

Welcome

You come through the gate,
and your life on earth begins:
light wavering green into the hue
of early spring, the growing
heat pouring leaf into form
just as you did, are doing, will do
with scarcity, rain, rivers,
kisses, wind, and horizons
that come each turning of the day.
You stand up in your dream,
lean on the fence, look wide
toward the stars just beginning
to burn through the sky
that carries the world.
A thunderhead powers upward,
spends itself over the past.
You take it all in, welcome
as rain in the tall reach
of the weather holding
this body of earth.

March 28, 2012: Chase County, Kansas. Receding supercell. I often pass this gate and make a mental note to place it in the foreground of a storm. On this day I visited the spot twice. My first try at the photograph failed because mid-level clouds obscured the back-building anvil. On my second attempt the mid-level debris cleared and revealed a sunlit anvil top. I have many Great Plains landmarks like this gate filed away in memory just waiting for the proper juxtaposition of storm and ground features.

April 4, 2009: Effingham, Kansas. Mammatus cloud. In early spring most severe weather storms are moisture-starved because the storms lack humid air from the Gulf of Mexico. In this photo the dew points are low and insufficient to make truly tornadic supercells. Yet a receding non-severe thunderstorm will often yield a golden mammatus cloud, particularly at sunset. I was also attracted to the lush green of the fresh wheat crop. I shot this scene before I drove home after a frustrating day of not seeing the supercells I expected. This shot was my consolation prize.

Panorama

This weather will not stop.
You watch the sky and remember
giving birth for the last time,
your view through the window
only of the darkness that leveled stars
and street light, your body like air
trembling in time with your pain.
Nothing could stop the power of life loving life
until the milky daylight set everything right,
burning through fog and time.
A newborn slept in your arms,
and the would-be thunderstorm exhaled
all directions: a dizzy of dark, light,
and the green fire of the world
while you fell back to sleep.

The panorama of a life filled your view
as it does now, as it could at any moment:
the angles of glory, the collapse of clouds,
the grief in rain shadow, the fragment of rainbow
—all exposed like you have always been,
all coming into form like the 18-year-old son
as well as the newborn he once was.
Across the expanse of a life, wake up
to the silver clouds and greenest fields,
everything held in the arms of space,
which cannot stop.

Step Out of Your Own Way

So easy to forget how to walk through your thoughts,
letting the weather in your head erase
the weather threading itself, right now,
through the trap lines of the wind, and the tunnels
of quiet between the rushing grasslands.
So simple to stop seeing what time wants to show you.

On the edge of the train's call, a whistle
half lost in the merciful sweetness of the wind
that conveys the stories of sky as large as your heart,
or what your heart can learn once you start walking
this tattered day, strong and fragile enough
to let each white song of lightning show you what's true.

April 8, 2011: Kaw Lake, Oklahoma. Outflow dominant supercell, cloud-to-ground lighting. This storm is tornado-warned (potentially capable of developing a tornado), but is now at the end of its tornadic life cycle and mostly producing rain. As the storm was pushed east by the cold outflow, it developed a horizontal shelf cloud. Because of low dew points, the storm didn't produce any tornadoes. However, the vegetation was brown and tinder-dry, allowing lightning to ignite grass fires.

April 14, 2012: Langley, Kansas. Tornado (above and right). I spent the entire day working this storm. It struggled with itself for hours trying to maintain two updraft towers, and I nearly abandoned it for alternative storms developing upstream. Then I felt the parameters were improving and had a sense this storm would become better organized with a single updraft, eventually producing a tornado. I lost my computer data so chased this storm "old school," using visual cues only. Because this storm was indeed the perfect form—cycling predictably and producing

multiple tornadoes—I was able to place myself in the proper position to capture this image. This tornado was one of over a hundred in Kansas, Oklahoma, Nebraska, and Iowa this day. Kansas took the brunt of the tornadoes, many poised to go through some of the state's largest cities, but amazingly, all the cities were spared, and there were no Kansas fatalities. Woodward, Oklahoma, however, was hit head-on, resulting in the deaths of five people.

Respect the Storm of the Storm

Watch like your life depends on it.
The first wave pushes the blackbirds
over the seam of the darkening west.
Uplifting wind multiplies and divides the world.
Flags tatter themselves in its speed. Then sirens.

From the overhang of your porch, wait
for the imprint of lightning to open your eyes.
Surrender to the wide yawning of thunder, the tendrils
trailing the supercell, and the one sweet songbird
at once unaware and aware. Follow
the storm of the storm, not the storm you expect.

When the rotation makes landfall, go inside swiftly.
Rush the stairs to the basement, grabbing the small cat
and photo albums on the way. Call the neighbors
from the crawl space. Press the anxious dog to your chest.
Turn up the weather radio and let the tone of danger
vibrate through your beating heart.

Obey the hunter you once were thousands of years ago.

April 22, 2010: Goodnight, Texas. Tornado and parent supercell. Look closely, and you will see the tornado below this supercell. This image gives a sense of how small a substantial tornado is when compared to the overall structure of the parent storm. This supercell was the second of two that moved through the area, both tornado-warned, but I favored this newer southern storm. It was more likely to produce a tornado than the northern storm because it had better access to unstable southerly surface winds. Storms like this are often called "Tail-end Charlies."

Goodnight, Texas

Goodnight, Texas, land of expanse and loneliness,
where the sky makes up in height for whatever is missing
in width. Goodnight, tumbleweed and stubborn blue
against the landscape of cloud. Goodnight, billowing light
and speed, the turning away from and toward that spawns
one errant tornado across the home of sage and javelina.
Goodnight, snakes pouring themselves underground,
and glistening vultures, cleared out ahead of the front.
Goodnight, cobalt sky tipping darker as it rises
rain and reflecting pond, where all stories reveal themselves.
Goodnight, old story of old weather, and waking panorama
of what's to come. Goodnight to the whitest clouds,
edged with momentum, and the myriad angles of gray,
surging ahead with danger tucked into their folds.
Goodnight, everything ready to vanish.

Hello, rising stars on the clearest night sky the coyotes ever saw.

What the Sky Is Made Of

The sky is made of soft rain and hard light,
the old yearning to be held, the ancient fear of not
having enough, and the fountain of wind that says,
Something's gone, something else is arriving.

The sky is made of rocks shattered finer than
the smallest atoms of human memory, air we call breath
once we take it in and turn it to motion, anger, or song.

The beating of hummingbird wings compose the sky,
as well as the fluttering of muscle on muscle, the space
in between the rain, the drum of the jackrabbit's heart.

The sky is made of rivers before and after they become rivers.

April 26, 2009: Canadian River, Roll, Oklahoma. Rope-out phase of the first of two tornadoes. The newer larger Canadian River tornado is developing in the large white wall cloud lower right. The deep blue color in the background is the result of the rear flank downdraft, which cuts into the mesocyclone. This opens up a slot in the clouds and allows blue sunlight to shine through.

April 26, 2011: Richland Chambers Reservoir, Texas. Outflow dominant supercell and shelf cloud. When storm-chasing, the objective is to get as close as possible to the storm, but sometimes, the view from further away is better, particularly in this shot, where the waves echo the lines in the storm.

Let the Rivers Clap Their Hands

Let the rivers clap their hands
over limestone outcroppings,
the gossamer of pin oak leaf
on the surface of water
while the watching sycamore
buds into tomorrow.

Let the rivers underground,
guarding their wares
or mourning the lack of turtles
dig new curves past old bends.

Let this motion make new lines
on the earth from thunder and time
in all the rivers we live,
all the rivers we are.

The Light In Between

Sharpens and softens the horizon
as if it isn't the space between
inhalation and exhalation,
knowing one thing, then forgetting,
or the split second of lightning
antiquing the sky. What we notice
last, if at all. The light in between
holds the house, the tree, the meaning
we make from furrowed field and supercell,
dying father and hospital window,
the threat to come and the yearning
to plant something anyway.
It shows us how to move from lack
and with purpose, gives us the strength
to climb back up from the basement
where we waited for the storm to pass
so we can brew some tea, take in
the carnival glass bowl of the sunset,
saved again, and step outside
to whatever life actually is.

April 29, 2009: Matador, Texas. Supercell over furrowed field. I was on my knees to make this picture of a supercell at the end of its tornadic lifecycle. Those deep furrows created fantastic leading lines and a vanishing point to an abandoned farmstead while the light was raking across the top of those furrows. I traveled tandem with this storm as it moved through Texas ending the chase in Matador.

April 30, 2009: Foss Lake Supercell, Oklahoma. This chase was nearly a "cap bust," which means storms were almost unable to break through the cap after a long day of warm and humid conditions. I had waited hours under the hot sun, and feeling dejected about getting any good shots, I started toward home. That's when I realized over my shoulder an updraft tower had penetrated the cap and was unleashing a tremendous amount of energy. High instability storms like this often produce tremendous lighting. The thunder from this storm had a unique sound, less like rumbles and more like bombs going off across the lake.

Supercell

for Stephen

Did you think your life was straight as this road,
something that could be time-lapsed into a predictable gait?
Do you try to map lightning, predict when
the thunderhead will pause and fold in on itself?
Have you pointed to a place in the clouds and said, "there"
just before it turned into somewhere else?
It is all nothing, then supercell, multiple strikes through
the clouds while the tips of the grass shimmer.
From the deep blue that narrates your life
comes the pouring upward of white curves and blossoms.
From the dark comes the thunder. Then the violet flash.
From the panorama of what you think you know
comes the collapse of sky, falling on you right now
whether you're watching the weather or not.
The world dissolves, reforms. What comes surprises,
motion moving all directions simultaneously, like the losses
you carry, talismans strung through your days, singing
of those you've loved deep as the blue framing the storm.
It rains for a moment in the field, in your heart,
then the weather stretches open its hand and says,
Here, this whole sky is for giving.

Finding the Moon

Did you stop now that you found
the moon almost full, floating west
across a small clearing between the clouds?
Did you still yourself in the lawn chair
on the deck and give up, waiting for one desire
to name itself, or another to dissipate?

Where have you been, the beautiful world asks.
Wind furrows your hair. The moon folds under
a cloud the size of a great lake. The light leaves
in increments. Lightning bugs thread their stories
through the cedars, which hold all seasons,
whether witnessed or not. The deep charcoal
of the windy night blows through you.

Then the moon rolls slowly back out,
a flashlight looking for you.
Why have you spent yourself ignoring this?

May 5, 2011: Monument Rocks, Kansas. Mid-level warm air advection streaming north at night. A severe weather setup was evolving for western Kansas, and warm moist air was advecting (a mass, horizontal movement) from the Gulf of Mexico. This advection translated visually into mid-level clouds traveling north over the Monument Rocks. A 30-second exposure recorded these streaming clouds as white streaks overhead. This photo illustrates the setup a night before severe weather. The following day, there were storms that produced copious amounts of hail, requiring snowplows to clear I-70 in Eastern Colorado.

May 15, 2009: Wellington, Kansas. Shelf cloud (underside). As shelf clouds often do, this one was traveling at highway speeds and I was struggling to stay ahead of it—a horse race between the storm and me. When I reached the town of Wellington, I was compelled to photograph this image, so I let the storm get ahead of me. As the storm passed over, it "cored" me, a storm chaser term for when the core—the center of the storm where there's the most intense precipitation—passes over the chaser. I got soaked, but I was glad to get this photo. A landmark such as this takes a generic storm cloud and gives it a real sense of place.

Wellington Water Tower

Lighthouse of the prairie
Herder of the traveler clouds
Top hat to the visiting circus
Wallflower at the big dance

Memorial for the dearly-beloveds
Welcomer to all life on the wing
Early riser to the dissolving dark
Flamenco dancer of the setting sun

Extreme sport for the young at heart
Standard-bearer for the four directions
Forefront for the mammatus backdrop
Delinquent of the darkness

Perspective to the shooting stars
Planet to the charm of goldfinch
Lantern for the lost and weary
Sailboat in the sky's vast sea

The bridge is made of weather. The bridge is made of time.
Translucent, the color of water, it spans the world in sharp relief
to lushness of green, western edge of blue, rain shadow in between.

Five miles north, the cedars drink up the storm while the sky inhales
old starlight, already dead when it lands, for rock and root,
bowed thunderhead and nightfall, velocity and cricket song.

The bridge is a slim path between dusk and longing, a wide swath
from sleep to starlight, an arm of weather linking here and there,
telling us that reality is always round, circling everything back.

The first lilt of lullaby, and beforehand, the roar of the bloodstream,
the steady clip of your mother's heart above where your own forms,
the tumble and turmoil out, ready or not, to the sharp light of birth.

The bridge arches itself past endings, showing us love is a wheel
that already knows what we learn: nothing is safe in this world
except change, courage, and the willingness to cross over.

May 19, 2013: North of Tonkawa, Oklahoma. Rain curtains and gust front. Like window treatment, sheer rain curtains create a wispy veil between the viewer and the setting sun. I wanted to capture the precipitation backlit against the bright western sky. Shortly after capturing this image, I was hit by strong wind and rain. My camera, tripod, and I got very wet before I could retreat to the vehicle.

May 19, 2010: Perry, Oklahoma. Receding supercell, mammatus cloud. The setting sun behind me illuminated this classic example of mammatus clouds in a receding supercell. The water in the foreground afforded me the opportunity to capture these reflections as well. The silvery cloud textures compelled me to render this image in black and white. This photo is the finale of a long day of storm chasing in Oklahoma.

What Do You Believe In?

The road, and the tumbleweed that follows it,
the night falling and the stars rising, the last
coherent thought, and especially what comes next.
The brown eyes of the dog when thunder shakes
the room. The wooden stairs from the house
where I grew up leading to the one where I live now,
my mother's laughter on the phone, the sudden falling
in a dream before waking, the dark made by thing
on thing, the chance smile of a stranger in the
grocery aisle, my youngest son's hand in mine
as he leads me down the hall, the threshold that
dissolves when I walk outside, the cranes stenciling
the sky behind the one leaf just breaking from the tree,
all the trees that turn light into something else,
a bluebird quick past the window, a secret pond
to gather at in our dreams, where all is forgiven,
all manner of water, arms wide open,
breast plate leading into the wind,
a lifting of the uncontainable
out of the contained.

Enraptured

They said this would come: an ending
to begin what comes next, but only
for the chosen at the precise moment.
Instead and always, this: the fire in the breath,
the blue-black horizon of the next storm,
the scent of rain, lost chances, and the inverse ocean
of sky. All of life opening its hands to show
that there is no place better than the crescent of now
bending around the earth, no place sweeter
than where thunderheads power grass and leaf.
We have this ending, this beginning, this falling
and lifting as we pound down the old cement stairs
to wait in the basement, or open back out the screen
door to see the reborn blue, the dance of what glows
and darkens, the return that cannot be reduced
to a billboard proclamation, the last ember
on the horizon, the first star, the second.

Look up. Look down. The world is
enraptured, and the world is where we live.

May 19, 2011: Cunningham, Kansas, rear flank of a receding outflow dominant supercell. A rouge preacher predicted the rapture to occur on May 20, 2011. This prediction was on my mind as I set out to photograph severe storms in central Kansas. I had hoped I would perhaps be blessed with an opportunity to photograph, if not the end of the world itself, something that was reminiscent of the end of the world, and lo and behold, the setting sun created a fiery red in the sky and imparted a glow to this storm that dwarfed the farm place.

May 19, 2011: Cunningham, Kansas. Receding supercell. My philosophy is: be somewhere at sunset. This maxim reminds me to be set up and ready to capture the quality of light that renders ordinary subjects in a wonderful way. In this case, it adds shadows and depth to the wheat field and clouds. It also mixes subtle pinks and reds with whites and blues. The storm punctuates the scene with lightning to complete the picture.

Celebrate This Kansas

Celebrate this sky, this land beyond measured
time that tilts the seasonal light. Dream the return
of the stars, the searing rise of summer or fast spread
of thunderheads, the secret-holding cedars and
witness rocks that migrate across the prairies.
We breathe the air of those who spoke languages
forgotten as the glaciers. We walk the fields
that once fed the fish of inland oceans.
We turn our heads away from where the raccoon
hid his family from the storm hundreds
of generations beforehand. This rain was once
a man's last wish, this heat what warmed a weathered
rock enough for a woman to rest on with her baby,
these fossils, love songs of memory and longing
after the beloveds die. This horizon the homeland
of butterfly milkweed oranging in ancient sun.
This creek's trail rerouted by deer and wild turkey.
This wooded curve the one favored by bluebirds
following last summer south. All we see,
the ghost and angel of billions of trails
through grasslands, the remnant of hard rains
where the grandmothers and grandfathers sang
of weather and loss, wars and births.
The bones of this land and the feathers of this sky
know us better than we know ourselves.

Then It's Over

The blue breaks through
the setting clouds, an old fire,
while the field lays down
its colors for the night.
Sky tumbles over itself
day to night, tension to calm.
What we think happened,
and what no one but the wind saw—
all lost to the first falling star.
Nothing hurts for a moment.
Those you love shine
whether still here or long gone.
A wide darkness envelopes
the world, takes your hand,
shows you where to stop
looking and where to start.

May 19, 2013: North of Rozel, Kansas. Sunset and clearing storm. I made this image at sunset minutes after the Rozel, Kansas, tornado. No lives were lost. The sky began to clear, and the wheat crop received new rain. Everything was returning to normal.

May 20, 2011: Topeka, Kansas. Tornadic supercell. This sculpted supercell surprised me because it occurred on a low-risk day. It traveled directly through the heart of Topeka, Kansas, and produced a funnel cloud over the city. In this image, the storm cycled and formed a new rotating rain-free base northeast of Topeka. I ran down into the field, very nearly on my knees, and waited until that little cloud notch moved into the break in the trees on the horizon.

What Would Happen If You Walked Here?

What would happen if you opened to something
so totally beyond human that it dissolved your borders
into bluestem? What if it rained and you got wet?
What if you understood not just that the earth tilted
but that it tilted right through your spine
and that's why you occasionally fall over?

Nothing prepares you for the real.
There's no journey out of this except the one
that separates your bones from your thoughts,
your tendons from the lines of your desire.

In the giant mouth of the dark,
in the opening screen of the dark,
in the bottom of the pot of the dark,
is the dark that isn't so dark.

In the myriad call of meadowlark layered on siren
of coyote upon clanging of wind in cottonwood tree
is also the sound of no sound, too.
Nothing can prepare you for the speed of the universe.
Nothing can steady you enough to absorb even the fact
that light travels millions of years to get to your eyes,
that the dissolved dust of stars are your thoughts
and your thinking, that the sky is so big,
that the dirt is made of bones and breath,
that there's nothing heavier than the sea,

that there's no such thing as exact
replicas in the seasons, and that seasons pour through us
like rain or dust whether we're paying attention or not,
that a rabbit can outrun you in your prime, that language
is only partially made of words, that the earth cannot help
but to keep recycling you into something better.

Dead End

The wind stops here
where land slopes up
to the clamor of clouds.
The animal of the sky paces
in its cage, looking for a way
that will only come with time.
The luster of tree tops already
knows there is no surrender
without risking everything.
What falls away will feed
the roots of what is:
the carefully tended grass,
the wavering afternoon,
the need for answers,
the end of the gravel.
It's the usual way we arrive
anywhere. No umbrella or map.
No way to get found
without getting lost first.

May 20, 2011: Perry Lake, Kansas. Supercell. I am always watching for ground features that will interplay with a storm. This quirky sign is all the more interesting against the updraft base of this supercell thunderstorm. May 19 and 20 storms were part of a larger upper air system that ultimately produced the Joplin tornado, on May 22, 2011, which killed 160 people and destroyed approximately 2,000 commercial buildings and 7,000 houses.

May 23, 2010: Tecumseh, Nebraska. Outflow dominant supercell and hail core. The clouds opened just enough to allow the western sunlight through, painting the storm with both warm and cool colors. At first this was a somewhat disappointing chase in that the storms were not particularly tornadic, but the light was so wonderful that I felt as though I was driving through a painting with luscious color. Overall, I spend more time running from and dodging hail cores than I do dodging tornadoes because virtually every big supercell has a hail core, and you can see a distinct hail core in this photo.

Convergence

The light turns itself over
to the peace of all we cannot see
while the road exhales dust, inhales
the car over the horizon of wet pavement,
the rain-saturated grass, the rushing
pink light, and the black cows
eager at the barbed wire.

This sky remakes itself in the sweep
of night and change over the next crest,
where another convergence encompasses
storm or calm, dog or car, vulture or thermal
the vulture rides. Dreams wheel over
the sleeping houses. Wind rocks
 Orange and rooftops.

Ahead, always a vanishing point
where sky and earth disappear each other,
the exact spot of the diving nighthawk,
the motorcycle down the road,
and all else we hear from the back deck.
What are we waiting for?

Seeing In The Dark

Barn's burnt down
now
I can see the moon
    —Masahide, 1657-1723

After the fire, what next?
Not the old words, aged with bitterness
or despair. Not habitual regrets and griefs.
Not just a reflection of anyone's ideas.
But what's right here: wind rising
through a tower of cottonwood.
Cicadas motoring their 17-year song.
Golden moon half revealed by
the silver of the passing cloud.

Good things, bad things happen.
News dissolves our vision of the world.
Not to say what's lost doesn't make us ache
or strip our days of reds so vibrant
we forget what we were thinking.

But whatever is lost also brings us to this window
composed of lush darkness, the rush or rain
through the leaves, the sudden chill dissolving
the hot anger or anguish, the pain of the questions
that, left unanswered, might divide us.

The music of the old house outlives the house.
We will make new murals out of the ruins,
mosaics from all that's broken, stone soup
at the center of our next feast.

Nothing in this world vanishes.
Even ghosts, loved enough, turn into angels.
The dark shows us what calls
not at the edge of what we sense
but from the center of where we live.

Nothing can take away the power of the real.

May 23, 2011: Kaw Lake, Oklahoma. Moonrise before tornado outbreak. Our eyes can play tricks late at night, and I thought I saw the image of a witch in this cloud at 2:30 AM. This turned out to be the night before a big tornado outbreak. This imagined omen gave me a sense that tomorrow would be a wild day. It did indeed turn out to be.

May 24, 2010: West of Broken Bow, Nebraska. Mammatus cloud. The Sand Hills of Nebraska were so wild and stunningly beautiful that I was unable to leave this spot. I stood there shooting pictures in every direction until it was too dark to see. This long storm chase, which took me hundreds of miles from home, led me to an area with a poor road network, which made it hard for me to keep up with these fast-moving storms (there was a 90-knot jet stream aloft). So I let the storm go to find out what the setting sun had to show me.

The Woman Who Watches the Sky

for Joan Foth

The woman who watches the sky knows how light
never slips but lands with intent, whitening into our view
what the earth says now when cedars rush east, the red
and rock pigments into history. No distinct categories
of the known and unknown but how they turn together
to bring new birds, a long diagonal of stratus,
and the mountain sharpened by steel blue clouds.
Lower down, poplars send up their yellow call,
shadows of one bend in the earth cover another,
and the road roots back to the slow green of memory.

It could be just west from Chimayo, or across the Flint Hills
of Kansas where the green turns red, the sky collapses.
It could be the weather, always vertical despite how we
move or age. It could even be night on the cusp of change,
the mourning doves emptying themselves of song,
the darkness that clamored for our anxious hearts
dissolving rain into the valley behind the next hill.

She hears the birds. She sees the bands of blue or wine,
the tilting flight of what's beyond our stories, and time's old clock
turning back to ground. When the sky comes, she's ready
for what any given moment of light and change sings
in its rusty voice of who she is, who she's always been.

Where the Road Ends

I've been here before. So have you.
The moment after the big fight, windblown
out of what to say next while all around us,
the wet green fields mirror the ocean of the sky.

There's only so far you or I can go
before we lose sight of the story we believe,
the past no longer a map for the weary,
the future too far below the cusp of horizon.

This is where the road ends.
There's nothing to do but walk,
the broken-down car left miles behind.
The polished air cups your face
when you look toward the sun,
balancing in the fresh blue of the after-storm.
The wind is a quiet feather, falling through
the space between us. Whatever we feared
is only tumbleweed, so why fear it?

Especially now when I touch the top of your hand,
you turn over your palm to hold mine.
You don't have to know where you're going
to be willing to go.

May 24, 2010: West of Broken Bow, Nebraska. Mammatus clouds. I was on a lonely stretch of highway in the Nebraska Sand Hills, and only saw about one car an hour. The mammatus clouds were moving in an interesting way and the sun on the horizon illuminated the bottom portion of the clouds with warm, golden light. The cool blue emanated from above and gave this photo a contrast of warm and cool colors.

May 24, 2011: Perry, Oklahoma. Night sky following tornado outbreak. After a large tornado outbreak in Oklahoma left a 50-mile-long trail of damage and killed eight people, the storm clouds cleared, and the moon and stars emerged. My campsite was littered with tin, roofing, and sundry debris that had been lofted 18,000 feet and traveled 60 miles. Earlier this day, I had a near miss with one of the storms. I was heading into Guthrie from the west to get ahead of the storm when I got an uneasy feeling. Although I couldn't see anything, I was driving into a rain-wrapped tornado. I had to stop, back up a quarter-mile west, and wait for a precipitation core to pass. Then continued my progress east where I shortly discovered a house that had been wiped out by the tornado. I was glad my instincts told me to stop when I did.

After the Storm, the Stars

Rise from the Osage orange, wheeling overhead as if nothing
has changed in the fresh heart of the air, cleansed free
of all but wind without end, lashing leaf against leaf.

The rays of remnant clouds burn translucent. Exposed dirt
ages in the wind. The grass tangles a slat from a child's doll cradle.
Paper from two towns away lifts to ferry important words nowhere.

The sky exhales, waits, drops to the disturbed ridge where flowers
rock upside down, the pebbles from elsewhere dream of the old days,
and in the off-and-on cadence of a train's whistle, someone cries.

Tomorrow, not so far from here: search dogs and careful lifting
of sheetrock and broken furniture, bulldozers, power saws, rented U-hauls
to unearth, sort, dry out and save, then clear, whatever's left.

Months ahead to measure what was lost, calculate this day's weather
and read the Braille of the stories left behind. The new world not conjured
arrives here anyway, and over this sprawling tree of life, the stars.

You Rise Up To Meet the Falling World

Whatever you lift to the sky, the sky covers:
middle-of-the-night exaggerations dissolve
to slivers of sadness on your pillow,
middle-of-life jolts compress the heavens
into one streak of sleet, thawing into softer ground.
Like the rain cycle that obscures the view,
you can lose your way on old ground or forget
the innate blue light in everything, ready again.
The surface of the tall grass spins in the breeze
it swirls into existence. The present twists down
to meet you each time you catch your foot.
Stars inform daylight or its absence.
We are made to catch the falling world,
just as the earth is shaped perfectly to catch us.

May 25, 2012: Victoria, Kansas. Rear-flank downdraft / inflow jet. This unusual storm feature is not a tornado. The rear-flank downdraft merged with a gusty dirty inflow jet lofting it overhead. At the time, I was shooting time-lapse on a tripod when the storm slammed me, and I had to retreat. Driving through it, I experienced zero visibility.

May 27, 2012: North of Hays, Kansas. Supercell sunset. The sky was filled with light during this magnificent sunset after a day of making time lapses of storms with very high bases as they streamed northeast on the dry line. Although storms were moisture-starved, storm structure improved as the day evolved. It turned out to be a great chase of a marginal setup.

Finding the Question

Is it the wind from the cedars
brushing the wet ground,
the nests of the wrens
tucked into the rock's eve?
Is it the storm over the horizon
willing the dark night
to lighten with change?
Is it the land across the lake
or the rocking of the canoe?
Is it the slim river I dream of, east
of the house where I grew up?
Is it my father's voice just before
he died, saying, What can you do,
or the weight of yearning I carried
before I knew I could put it down?
Is it the way I lift my arms over
my head to give up or ask for help?
Is it god or the ceiling fan, nightfall
or the wheeling of stars behind stars
shivering me here tonight?
Is it the love for the earth
I didn't know I was?

Your Road

Walk down your road while darkness
shadows away fields.
Broad sun, at the end of its day,
antiques the horizon.
Each step you take reverberates
on underground riverbeds
that tumble root and death
into dirt and heat. Overhead,
the river of clouds widens,
illuminating the line of your road,
which is never just a way from or to,
but a border, an arrow, a seer,
a container, a hunch, a ballad
about fear, love, and pacing,
and how much you are
what the ground holds: secrets
worn as bleached bones under
the cedars. Your heart storied
as the redbirds that burst like confetti
from the braided branches
of the interior. Take another step,
let your road go far from you,
become what leads and is led at once.
A turning flock of blackbirds,
a shush in the wind, a hand
on your left shoulder telling you
that you are never alone.

May 27, 2013: North of Hays, Kansas. Clearing storm clouds. After a disappointing and unfruitful storm chase in northern Kansas, I turned my truck around to face the long drive home.

May 30, 2011: Odessa, Nebraska. Receding supercell, mammatus clouds, intra-cloud lightning. While storm chasing in the Nebraska Sand Hills, my engine began making a terrible noise, and I was forced to end my day and find refuge for the night. Whatever was going on with my engine sounded quite severe so my goal was to limp back to civilization. This truck stop ended up as my port, quite literally, in the storm. Although distraught about circumstances and worried about my engine I could not ignore the sky drama atop this bustling truck stop. The mammatus and lightning intrigued me so I made this image before spending the night in my broken truck.

All Night at the Truck Stop

Close your eyes, but no use:
the motor of storm
trucks down the highway
igniting opposing splashes.
Too much coffee all day
dream-blurs spilled neon
and gas pumps, white beacons
of salvation for the weary.
Flashes irregular but relentless.

Far away, over the ridge of weather,
past the moment in its rusty frame
as a lost night with found lightning,
there will only be time-lapse stories
of a truck stop you drive by,
days scattered over the field of the future,
without remembering.

But now, before the river of decades
streams across the wet pavement,
there is this: *Wait here,* the rain says.
The tumble of thunder.
The pause between the pause,
adjusting your life.

The Crossroads in Every Step

We breathe in intersections, taking in here,
exhaling there: memory and physiology,
myth and heartwood, daring leap and long sleep.
Peace spreads itself into a recognizable shape--
leaves, the sky between, and mostly the falling
that feeds the base of this tree, the start of another.
The world is made of glimmer and tatters,
the light left by one for another, the dull shine
of mid-afternoon on the driveway gravel,
the iridescent car's reflection in the side-view mirror.

No place that isn't an intersection: you're born out of
two people's meeting, you die by at another crossroads.
No center that's not edge, no time that's not all times,
what you've lived petaling out, what you're living
rooting down, what you may live over the eastern horizon,
a kind of weather that might organize itself into a storm
or fall apart as the blue sky bleeds through.
No matter what happens, the air will be different.

The dragonfly lands on your palm or not.
Nothing ever to hold but this need for holding.
You think you're moving through, but actually
the convergence is moving you.

May 28, 2013: North of Russell, Kansas. Mammatus clouds at sunset. What does it mean to have a spiritual experience? In my case, it is the felt experience of absolute presence, simultaneously big and small, when the self is forgotten. This sunset was the grand finale of a perfect chase. I had photographed the now legendary Bennington, Kansas, tornado earlier in the day.

June 4, 2010: Colorado High Plains. Mammatus cloud. The Colorado High Plains is an arid landscape, typically very brown except in June, which is the month for peak rainfall. I arrived here sleep-deprived after leaving Kansas City at 3 AM and driving until afternoon. All of a sudden, I began to feel faint, and I realized I had been up for more than 24 hours, hadn't eaten properly, and was hitting some kind of fatigue and low-blood-sugar wall. I then remembered an energy bar at the bottom of my gym bag, which I now think of as the energy bar that saved my life. Within a few minutes of eating it I was replenished, my attention returned to the storm and I made this image.

Beginner

Where is that heart,
the center of the field
swung open by the wind,
so we can see what's
still wet and ready to unfurl?

Where's the ledge? Where's the grief
that tears apart all the fencing?
Where's the sudden quiet
when the light through the cedars
dissolves shadows, and the grasses
ignite against the changing dirt?
Where's the exact location
where no answers matter?

What does it mean to inhale
this surrender, to exhale into
the sky that holds up
twisting charms of goldfinch
and battered clouds, ready
to change into something else?
How do I bend to get there?

Being Made of Weather

You have no idea what you're capable of.
The rotation born of two opposing forces can
explode down Main Street in any town, any mind.
Fight the front moving through?
Give up and sleep through the storm?
Choices as if they are choices when it's time
to ask yourself what you're ready to give up,
and what you can save: dead photos, living animals,
a tea cup from great-grandmother, a pink-gray
arrowhead found in the rocks along an Ozark lake
in 1983 when someone taught you to skim stones.
Mostly, the hand of the child you lead into the cellar.
Mostly, your own heartbeat, audible as hard breath,
which you must protect and give freely as light or water.
Always, the will to return the moment the storm
brings you back out to see what you're truly made of,
lift the fallen branch or plank, bend to call out a name,
your whole life waiting for the smallest of motion.

June 5, 2009: La Grange, Wyoming. Tornado. As I was quickly approaching the storm, I crested the hill and was stopped in my tracks by this vista. I elected to shoot the storm from this position, putting the town in my foreground. It appeared as if the tornado was going to come straight down Main Street. Ultimately it drifted south, and La Grange (population 332) was spared. Southeast Wyoming often has storms percolating along the Cheyenne Ridge due to a phenomenon known as orographic lift which occurs when rising terrain pushes up an air mass as it advects from a low elevation to higher elevation. This is why it often rains in mountains in the afternoon. The La Grange tornado is the most scientifically documented tornado in history. Vortex II, a research armada of ten mobile radars, including the Doppler On Wheels (DOW) surrounded this tornado and collected data during its 30-minute life cycle.

June 9, 2010: South of Alliance, Nebraska. Updraft tower, intra-cloud lightning. I lost blood to capture this picture at night in the middle of the Nebraska Sand Hills, one of the most mosquito-ridden places on earth. Mosquitoes attacked me mercilessly. Once the image was completed, I returned to my vehicle to get some relief but quickly discovered that it too was filled with mosquitoes. It made for a long night.

When the Brokenness Vanishes Before Your Eyes

It isn't what they told you, a fracture in the jaw,
or splinter in your finger that can never be removed.
Healing comes whether or not you're watching
in the falling-down house of the body that's upright enough
to live in most days. The old or the new can vanish,
leaving you amazed as you sit on a folding chair,
letting the sun and wind sideways clear you.

The girl you are, fire to fire, in the marrow of your bones,
can sit up unfettered on her colt legs, take your hand,
tell you, "Look, it doesn't hurt anymore."
The oldest woman you will be can lean her forearm,
still muscular, on your shoulder, and nod,
her eyes your most beautiful you never saw.

The dead cannot grip weapons anymore,
and the ones still here will lose interest eventually.
It's how the seasons land in each future glimpsed.
The pregnant woman you were can put her feet up,
laugh at the thousands of mosquito worries.
The father or mother, the brother who never said much,
the best teacher or worse friend parallel play.
Scars turns to landscape, bone regenerates itself,
the splinter slips out over time, the lost return home,
and the bad father begs forgiveness. Let yourself
be gathered up, broken to unbroken, in time.

June 10, 2010: Last Chance, Colorado. Waning supercell. I had been planning this shot for several years. Already familiar with the whistle stop town of Last Chance, I pre-visualized that sign with a supercell in the background. Minutes after documenting the tornado I rushed to Last Chance and was able to realize my vision.

June 10, 2010: Last Chance, Colorado tornado and harrier hawk. I love how the harrier in this image seems to command the sky in spite of the storm. I felt fortunate to catch the bird precisely in the correct position to make this a nice composition. Luckily harriers hover quite a bit, affording me time to get the shot. The tornado itself was not particularly dramatic, but the bird makes the picture.

Last Chance Tornado

One sturdy funnel spins
where no one but the voles live.
The deserted whistle stop of
Last Chance has only the wind's
stories: a hole in the cafe sign,
empty houses that once dreamed
of prosperity and fellowship
now shedding siding,
and for miles around, the dirt
trembling in its cradle,
newly planted, ready
for what comes. The updraft
tightens its lift, the wind
ripples the ground, turns up
limestones buried a century ago,
aches apart what time has bound
while a single harrier
ferries itself east, pulling
behind it the dark sheet of stars.

Not Rare But Precious

Think of what's not rare but precious.
—*Ruth Gendler*

The gift of light. Of dark.
The squeaky swing set
that's really a blue jay
searching for love and gravity.
What tells you to lie down.
Why standing back up
each morning is precious
as breath or clouds splintering
into rain dissolving the drought.
The horizontal day that turns
into the vertical night,
the stubble on the path
between the furrows of labor,
hope, and need. Any curve
wheeling toward the horizon,
all the dreams of finding
your house has extra rooms,
the ease of a broken love
suddenly making sense,
the return of a lost locket
from childhood, and in it,
your grandfather's face.
Waking this afternoon to
thunder, the smell of rain.

June 11, 2010: Colorado High Plains. Outflow dominant supercell over maturing wheat crop. I watch for lines on the ground that echo shapes in the sky. To get what I was looking for, I was forced to foot chase deep into this field to create this composition. That storm was outflow-dominant, another way of saying it was an old storm, falling apart or, as we like to say, "gone cold," and not particularly interesting anymore from a tornadic standpoint. Yet the ground features, especially the agricultural lines created by tractors, were interesting, so after hiking out a long way, I started taking pictures, trying to get the image of the cloud over the drainage path. I had to move fast because there was a lot of cloud-to-ground lightning.

June 12, 2010: Colorado High Plains. Petite arcus cloud. A cloud shaped like this is caused by cold outflow that undercuts the storm, lifting and flattening the updraft into a horizontal shape. In this picture, you can see the undercutting rain curtains behind the arcus cloud (often called a shelf cloud). Due to orographic lift, storms repeatedly formed on a geographic feature called the Palmer Divide giving me the opportunity to shoot multiple storms moving east. I stayed here much of the day and kept shooting these forms.

When the Rain Comes

The clouds roll in,
shadows holding up light,
titled silver at the edges.
Trees everywhere turned,
sidewalks dry and wanting,
grass silvering
in stalks of wind.
The branches heavy
with blackbirds,
the old wall of sky etched
with worn lightning.
The whole fields lifted
to the breaking world
where, for a moment,
all that wants to be said is heard.

Field Love

This love soars through me like italics,
like a chant, like rain into a pond
when I stand in this place:
the red grasses, or the black absence
after the fire, the first point of green
from the center of the earth.

In the morning, the deer sail across the window.
In the twilight, the slopes filter dark upon dark.
In the woods, too much undergrowth, too many
fluorescent green brains of Osage orange,
toward the nappy seams of the grass.
Beyond the woods, horizons never skittish,
dream of light tumbled recklessly everywhere.

When the wind pours up and over the top,
the light of day chills slightly. I lean over
the deck railing, over the feathering grass,
for once seeing—like stars surging out
from the blackening sky—the difference between
love, and the defense of love against itself.

June 12, 2010: Colorado High Plains. Rain curtain. These rain curtains help reveal the wind fields that fall vertically before changing horizontally when hitting the ground and forming a rain "foot." This image shows one in a sequence of storms that moved by me. Although it did become tornado-warned and produce a funnel, the funnel never fully condensed to form a tornado. However, the light was just right for a vivid photo.

June 14, 2013: West Point, Nebraska. Supercell. The now legendary West Point Supercell was nearly stationary as I set my camera on a tripod and fired away for 30 minutes never needing to recompose the image as the mesocyclone rotated in place. It might have continued another hour, but a much larger thunderstorm complex from the west consumed it during its prime.

Mercy. Daring. Courage.

I have three treasures which I hold and keep.
—Tao Te Ching

I carry my treasures close to my skin.
I walk carefully and fast, pause to glimpse
the lightning. So much fire compressed
makes the visible even more visible.
To see this is to know mercy, and how
it tumbles shards of glass and stone
to reconfigure this day. To know mercy
is to know daring: every molecule of love
so delicate and damaged, willing as grass
to fly backwards at high speed while lightning
flashes the veins of the heavens. To know
daring is to know courage, how it's equal parts
fear and will, rooted in the dense stillness
of the cottonwood banking the creek,
and the creek itself rounding the horizon
toward whatever comes, trials or treasures,
raining down to wake us up.

Coordinates

I live just south of the poetic,
where the glaciers stopped short, sloped down
to nothing. Now low-flying catfish line
the brown rivers while the valleys go flat
as clavicles edging into erosion and horizon.
The grass, obsessive as always,
runs itself oblivious,
and the cedar trees wave,
one arm, then another,
as if under water.

I live where the sky, dense and
exhausted, complains all smug and blue
that nothing ever happens here,
and leans asleep on its elbows in the corner.
It dreams what we mean: that we can only
locate ourselves in the weather that maps us
but can't be mapped ahead of itself.

Here there's no way to know what's coming,
or what's gone, the big bluestem as tall as it is.
The wind comes. The wind goes. The sun climbs
around the corner and returns at its appointed time.
The windows shake in the storm that can pick up
a field, undress it, place it back down.

When I try to say where I am, I can only
point to the rushing everywhere
the mind tries to be still,
and in that wind, the stillness
that holds a single glance of switchgrass
up to the light before letting it go.

June 15, 2012: Kanorado, Kansas. Shelf cloud at sunset. This is a very thin, low-precipitation, linear thunderstorm, so thin the setting sun behind shines through. There's maybe less than a couple miles depth to this storm. Although it is scary looking its bark is worse than its bite and not as dangerous as it looks.

June 15, 2009: West of Wellington, Kansas. Arcus cloud. Unidirectional wind shear and other factors caused multiple storms to quickly congeal into a line or what is also known as a Mesoscale Convective System (a complex of thunderstorms which becomes organized on a scale larger than the individual thunderstorms). This line developed the bowing structure. The storm was racing southeast at highway speeds. I placed myself in front of it just long enough for this picture. Shortly after this exposure, the storm slammed into me with 50-mph, straight-line winds, heavy rain, and hail.

Questions for Home

Did you imagine there was more than this?
More than the grass or the sky?
More than a six-year-old's quick touch of fingertips
on your sleeve? Did you believe it would add up
to a history of torrent and mathematics,
ultimate meanings, causes and effects
intersecting like constellations of the
greatest minds you never knew?

It's just a gravel road in the country.
An edge of grassland washed out of its redness.
It's just a bobcat you missed because you opened the door
a second too late. The breeze inside the breeze,
the dominant gait of weather, the green light in the distance.

Here, don't be afraid. It's not like you lost anything
but the craving for craving, and even that will return.
Where else would you rather be than right here
where the bluebird blurs past the cedars,
and time sheds its old skin so its new one can form?

June 15, 2009: North of Dodge City, Kansas. Supercell. The proliferation of wind farms makes a scene like this increasingly common. It is always visually fascinating to watch severe storms interact with turbines. I have always wanted to photograph a tornado near or in a wind farm, and this is the closest I have come. This storm did produce a tornado, but it was several miles east after it had passed the wind farm. I was wondering how the wind farm might be affected by a tornado, and I suspect the day is coming when a tornado will test the large blades on the turbines, probably breaking them off.

Chasing Weather

Unpredictable as love that will outlive us,
the clouds fold fast, twist themselves wide.

The supercell spins blades in rusty speed,
then leans to the west, sweetening its tune
by forgetting the melody. The taste of sun lingers.

Crows wait for the shadows the moon will throw.
Wind picks up its luggage, puts it down again
until there is nothing left to move.

What's gone seems gone for good no matter how often
the song returns, broken light reddening the horizon
like a heartbreak or a question we can never get over.

Time chases time. Dirt chases rain. Wind chases everything.
The weather finds us with ease, knowing from long ago
where we live, so why embark on the hunt for what
can never be caught? Let the dark of the dark find you.
Invite the weather in to chase its dreams inside your own.

Welcome

for Jane

Welcome to the state of wonder that hinges sky to field
where the sun tilts purple through the winter stratus,
and the road winds along the river bank for miles.

Welcome to floating dust on the air, cat on the bed,
squirrel on the bench, breath of the wind,
lantern for you in the center of your life.
Welcome to the color orange, bird song flooding
the stand of cedars, the shimmer of nightfall on rooftops.

Welcome to the living room couch, where you'll nap
one afternoon in July, and wake up in the sweet and wild
tunnel of cicada song. Welcome to your most tender grief,
past or future, opening the windows so you can feel
how much the life without is the life within. Welcome
to the clearing, where your beloveds sit invisibly
on the lichen-speckled rock, waiting to see what you do
with the air you take into your lungs.

Welcome, sapphire sky the sycamore branches hold,
softening ground that holds the roots, roots that hold
the whole world. Put your hand on the door knob
to the rest of your life chiming its welcome song
like water on rocks, wind on fields, moonlight on trees,
owls perched on the cusp of change, all singing,
welcome to your roundest joy.

June 17, 2009: Grand Island, Nebraska. Mesocyclone. This long-lived, tornadic supercell cycled through many phases prior to my making this picture. At one point the tornado warning was allowed to expire only to have it re-warned when the storm cycled up again. At this time, the supercell was strengthening and moving east where it would go on to produce the Aurora, Nebraska, tornado, which did do damage to a dogfood plant. Luckily, it lifted right before it entered Aurora, so the town of over 4,000 was spared.

June 17, 2009: Aurora, Nebraska. Backside of supercell, flanking inflow. This is the Aurora supercell after the tornado. From this angle, it looks like a mountain of agitated cloud and lighting. The storm was receding, and I was letting it go. Shooting the storm as it goes away is often rewarding because of how beautiful the backside of a storm can be.

Entering the Days of Awe

Let us walk unfettered into these days
of sun, wide fields of old grasses
bracketed by sunflowers and pebbles.
Let us step into the lapis sky that fastens itself
to the driveway, the sidewalk, the worn leaves
of dying summer under new leaf fall.

Let us give up the wasteful thinking,
the 2 AM anxieties over what cannot be changed,
the waking with a gasp. Let us stand in the morning,
the new chill of the air clearing remnants of time,
fear, reaching too hard or not enough.

Let the wrongs be made right. Let forgiveness
overtake the words we hear and pray, the stories
we've made and tilted. Let us remember this dreaming song
from all our beloveds long gone or just around the bend,
each note engraved with lost lands, singing
of how good it is when we dwell together.

Let the peripheral vision in the days of awe show us
the world, the first seeing of the heart, the last pulse
of those we love who travel with us. Let the wind shake
the trees, the tattered leaves shine, the last butterflies
flash their orange, the first dark blue of night
open into a panorama of past and present light
on its way to us all.

Let the next breath we take inscribe us in the book of life.
Let the next breath you give welcome us home.

June 17, 2010: West of Albert Lea, Minnesota. Conger tornado (above and right). The Storm Prediction Center logged 115 tornadoes in Minnesota and South Dakota. Four of the tornadoes rated EF4. I targeted southern Minnesota and photographed tornadoes continuously for two hours. I lost count of how many I witnessed, but I do remember seeing every size and shape, including multiple vortex tornadoes. Storms were moving slow and recycling on the warm front, so I was able to keep pace with them even after debris and blocked roads forced multiple detours due to all

the downed power lines and trees. I stayed safe by staying in the inflow notch, the part of the storm where the surface winds flow into the storm, typically southeast of a tornado. Yet I was continually looking over my shoulder for redevelopment. You have to be vigilant in these situations. In the end, the tornadoes destroyed several farmsteads and killed three people.

Right Before They Begin Again

They try to steady the disbelief in their eyes, their hands
over their mouths. She carries the baby on one hip
while he leads the toddler through what used to be home
before the sky turned everything inside out: love letters,
cushions, walls, cabinets, clothes forgotten, and somehow,
a porcelain ballerina, still dancing on a shelf.
Everything is water-damaged, or buried except for
the matter-of-fact retelling of holding tight to babies
in the root cellar while their house thrashed and flew.
They sort through numbness and paper, trying to make
quick decisions: save the doll with the broken face?
The single pearl earring? The only surviving plate?
Then there's another form to fill out, bags of clothes
the neighbor's daughter sent over, and at the end of the day,
chicken sticks for the kids, coffee and burgers for them
at the motel cafe while another stranger covers their bill.
In their dreams, walls mean something, and foundations
root sturdy as 100-year cottonwoods even the tornado misses.

June 19, 2010: West of Concordia, Kansas. Abandoned farmstead, outflow dominant supercell. Some images beg to be black and white, and this quintessential Kansas image was one of them. On this particular day, there had been a tornadic supercell with a tornado west of Concordia, but the storm was now becoming outflow-dominant, overly mature, and messy. Right after I took this picture, the rear downward flank winds struck me and nearly ripped the door off my truck. That door hinge is loose to this day.

What the Grasses Say

How is it you should love,
you who cannot say the word
without forgetting it is not yours
to keep silent as fallen leaf under foot?
How do you presume to speak for us?
We who filter wind as regularly
as you exhale, we who hide
all things made of fur
and engine hearts.
We who throw our lives
down without a thought,
who fling open at the roots
and cry in love with
the wind, the wind, the wind?
What do you even know of the wind
when your body can hardly ever
split apart, open at the seams
and pour back into a whole field
of singing grass?

June 19, 2011: Red Willow, Nebraska. Receding supercell, mammatus and intra-cloud lightning (above and right). The headlights failed on my truck, so I was forced to abandon the chase and quickly make camp on Red Willow Lake, Nebraska. Good thing as I was fortunate to witness one

of the most dramatic lightning displays of my life. This beautiful storm had some very interesting structure on the leading edge of it and some fantastic lightning, which led me to create my best time-lapse sequence and some of my best still images.

Rain

The wall of noise dissolves to rain,
a world held in place by a million falling threads.
In the balance, the fur on the coyote's belly,
worn as leather but marked with a lifetime of fights,
and the lake hungry for new stories to swim with the old.
Lightning angles and wishbones, branches into branches
that mimic what grows or tunnels below.

Scenery unrolls quick-silver—expanses of land
or water, sky and darkness—in the flash that lights up
all the lines of roads and clouds, cedars, and shorelines,
before sealing all back together in shifting hues of night.

What seems like the end, again is a beginning.
What can't be said, suddenly pouring down everywhere.

June 20, 2011: Bradshaw, Nebraska. Tornado. This storm was a unique setup. It was a cold core storm (in which the upper low center is on top of the surface low center) with access to substantial instability, resulting in a long track tornado. The tornado originally had a dark and dirty appearance, but toward the end of its life cycle, it was caught in a favorable light and became white. My good chase vehicle was in the shop for repairs, so I had to take my 20-year-old car with broken headlights, windows that didn't go up and down properly, no air-conditioning, and no way to mount a video camera. Luckily, I was able to get this great image anyway.

Surrender

Give up your house of chance, which was never yours
to begin with, and listen carefully for stillness and sirens.

Release the horses, and crack open the windows.
Gather the cats and dogs, babies and grandmothers.

Go underground and wait. Hear your pulse
and your tender fear as the house rattles.

Hold onto the others, your hand a messenger of assurance,
your eyes in the dark nodding to other eyes in the dark.

When you can't hear or see anymore, breathe.
When you can, climb up carefully.

Open the door to the white god rushing the ground ahead.
Your life glimmering in your chest. Grateful. Grateful. Grateful.

Return

Where have you been, my little one?
Junco on a far branch, tangled in bareness.
A fast parade of raindrops interrupt
the long diatribes of the mind on exactly
how to say it if it needs to be said at all.
The distractions become the main event
all the time the air is performing miracles.

Look: the naked storm has twisted itself into light.
Evening, then nighttime, hangs in the balance
of rows of winter wheat overcoming the horizon.
The wind sweeps clean the bare heart.
Everywhere, the tall reach of the sky returning
us home. No place a placeholder.

June 22, 2010: West of Goodland, Kansas. Tornadic supercell. Storms on the High Plains have been referred to as naked storms, meaning there are no mid level clouds to obscure the storm. An image like this is uncommon in the eastern states because of general cloudiness. This photo came after a long, fruitless chase. However, this storm developed right at sunset with an interesting structure and brilliantly clear air.

June 22, 2009: Goodland, Kansas. Mammatus cloud. After a storm has passed, I always look up. There may be an interesting mammatus cloud display directly above. The effect of the setting sun combined with a deeper blue color coming from above made for this image.

Speaking to the Wind

Where are you now when you're everywhere?
Jackrabbit of shadow, rustle of dry grass.
Then it's night, and you sweep through the center
of tree or field, your hands in love with what
your wrists do when dancing over 40 mph.

What unfolds its wet wings in the warm dark
only to be dried into flight by you?
What climbs a happy slope of light
up the walls of the sky, only to clang
down fast down to the earth where a dragonfly
holds tight to the paltry underside of leaf?

Where do you go when you leave us,
or is it that you never completely leave,
the shaking light and dimming dark always
on the move to fill in all the holes of the universe?

Last Night in June

Wind and leaves filter the heat.
A lightning bug stitches a straight line
over the roof. A dog barks, then stops.
Miles and days backwards or forward
south of here, waves hit the rocks of the shore,
tangling feathers and branches in the oil spill.
No one knows how to stop it. Severe weather
to the north spurs tornadoes, and a lifetime's
walk north of that, rivulets of water
finger-slim tunnels in the ice cap, melting
what's on the surface from far below.
The atmosphere clings to whatever it can find,
makes fronts and backs out of whatever comes.
The planet inhales, draws rain down to this
particular spot of young leaves and old wind
as the bolt strobes, cracking us open.

June 26, 2008: Salina, Kansas. Cloud-to-ground lightning. I shot this with a tripod-mounted camera on the shoulder of the road and operated the shutter from the relative safety of my vehicle using a remote controlled radio trigger to reduce the danger of deadly lighting. Shortly after shooting this, a strong wind gust nearly toppled my heavy tripod.

June 27, 2013: Tonkawa, Oklahoma. Arcus cloud with an attendant haboob (dust storm). This storm chased me from Wichita to the northern Oklahoma border. At Tonkawa, I stopped to photograph it as it was approaching me at 60 mph, and I only had a few minutes to make the photograph before the haboob hit me. I was soon swamped with dust and dirt, and visibility dropped to zero.

Imagine You Know How to Fly

In fact, you've done it all your life—
the view from above always multi-textured, dense,
promising more than close-ups.

Like this field, mid-summer, watercolor green.
Up close, the deer's contoured belly,
muscles straining against the underside of fur.
See how it breathes?

Now fly forward to the edge of late summer,
just a few fireflies diagonally making their way up
through the white air to blue air, thinning to a wisp.
Drop your arms and stop fighting.

Leave your house behind you.
Go to the wind pouring over and under
the ledge of the sky.
Jump in.

Do You Know Where You're From?

Do you know where the motion
originates in a field of big bluestem,
the single point where the fire began?
Have you looked for your origins
where the interstate belts the hills flat?
Do you count the trucks that read "Navajo,"
billboards promising comfort or salvation,
and cottonwoods crowding a dead river's
old bank? Are you willing to turn
from what's right in front of you
for what only risk and peripheral vision
will show you? Do you look carefully
into the shadowed woods for lost herds
that should be in the field,
and into dying supercells
for the cycles still churning?
Do you watch the light transmitted
from the wings of goldfinch?
Do you ask, each footstep a syllable,
how to walk the right story home?

July 12, 2010: Colby, Kansas. Dying supercell. An hour before, this storm was tornadic and rather threatening. Minutes after this image was made, it literally went "Poof!" and disappeared into blue sky. What was most interesting to me was how the storm died so abruptly. The updraft separated from the base while the remnant from the updraft went up into the jetstream and was carried away. The base of the storm hovered a few minutes, then vanished.

July 19, 2010: Princeton, Missouri. Back-building anvil, tornadic supercell. Whenever the top of this supercell reached a higher altitude, tornado or funnel reports would occur below. While I usually don't shoot in Missouri because of terrain, I went after this storm because it had been a while since I chased. I shot the storm from a distance because hills and trees did not favor a close perspective.

Blue

Light breaks down everything into time:
leaves into dirt, dirt into stone, stone into river,
river into roots, roots into a single pin oak tree
blown hard in the blue ache of the storm.
Your life changes to air, dust, lapping waves
of cobalt reflecting ongoing night,
silver dimming to gray in the ease of dawn.

A blue circus of joy and gymnastics rushes or slows
the clouds over rocks, interruptions, losses,
makes you stop your car at the end of your drive,
get out quickly, lift the dead bluebird from the gravel
—its inverse weight a sad gift in your hands—
while the blue of the blue takes over everything:
branches baring themselves, stalks of change translated
into grass, and the interior sky called thinking.

The Slant of Everything

Always just to your right,
an angle at sunset from the pilot light
of the clouds, or the slant of distant
lightning and crickets to echo humidity.
Sometimes everything lifted on sudden breezes,
surprisingly cold as they split the summer open.
The silver west slants past the horizon ahead.
The greening east bends its heat and insight
so that the wrong ideas can burn away
in air so thin that it no longer matters
who didn't choose you, or what you forgot.
The slant of everything tilts plans or wishes,
showing us, just as the western-leaning cottonwood
with its eastern-leaning roots, how the world
always rises two directions at once.

July 30, 2010: Kansas City, Missouri. Arcus cloud, cloud-to-ground lightning. The arcus cloud in this image appears to scrape the ground as it defines the intersection between cold outflow and warm unstable air. I photographed this storm in downtown Kansas City, from the bluffs overlooking the Missouri River. The storm produced this dramatic-looking shelf cloud, then moved to Liberty, Missouri, where its shape scared many people. A law enforcement officer contacted me after the fact, asking if it had been a tornado to which I replied, "No."

August 1, 2013: West of Mullen, Nebraska. Thunderstorm updraft base with lightning. I was deep in the Sand Hills of Nebraska, a largely uninhabited region with no radio stations, telephone, or internet data. Worst of all, there are few roads, making it hard to navigate. The area is untamed yet beautiful with wildflowers. The supercell above is marked by an updraft base on the right, and a bright luminous hail and precipitation downdraft on the left. The railroad track shot was planned: I set my camera on a tripod and patiently waited for lightning to align itself with the leading line of tracks. My lightning forecast verified, and this image is the result.

The Door of the Grass

for Beth

Where to go now that all roads dissolve?
How to follow deer paths or sudden partings
of big bluestem, little bluestem, switchgrass into
the field so deep that you can no longer see the edges?

No need to answer, says the wind. Just walk.
Just stop in this surprise of clearing
where some other has stopped before you.
Listen to the careful tremble, the heavier rushing
tumbling upward and out from the tops of
rusting rail tracks. Let it sweep back over you.
Your mind only blossom and stubble,
breaking against what you thought you knew
until it too blows free or roots deeper
into something like bedrock turning under us.

Here in the house of the grass,
wind tells the sea in you, the old stars in you too,
welcome home.

In Gratitude

The wind thanks you, unfurling over the worn
horizon so it can billow into night. The stars too,
whether talismans of light dying or just being born,
behind the small birds arriving or staying behind,
who balance gratefully on thin branches of coming winter.
The squirrel in the field, the hidden fox, the mammals
under and overground. The world is composed,
is composing itself anew even in a narrow time:
just before the red-winged blackbird folds
back in silhouette. Whatever act of kindness flies
lands in the heart of a moment, a seasonal marker
to illuminate why we live, a song of gratitude.

August 7, 2009: Kadoka, South Dakota. Thunderstorm updraft with back-building anvil at sunset. If storm photography was restricted to a front porch, I'd buy a house in Kadoka, South Dakota, because 100 miles west of Kadoka, small storms percolate on top of the Black Hills all day. If conditions are favorable, a strong storm will move east off the hills and travel toward Kadoka, sometimes becoming tornadic and backlit by the sunset.

August 7, 2011: Tuttle Creek Lake, Kansas. Cloud-to-ground lightning. I usually camp at night and try to select a location that will allow me to shoot overnight time-lapse photography without ruining the camera with rain. On this night, I camped south of a stationary front, allowing my cameras to shoot lighting storms from sundown to sunrise in a precipitation-free zone

Dancer

Don't wait in rooms, away from windows.
Instead, come to the porch, the overhang,
the wide eaves to wait and not wait anymore.
Even the cicadas are astonished into quiet
while the world cracks into one gesture
or another, calls in its sudden, low voice
of rumble and yawn for us to move
our shoulders, shake the sleeping heron
in our lungs awake, curve our hips
to invite the siren of the coyotes back.
It's time to find the balancing point
especially if falling is involved,
to let the animals of our bodies find
their stance: the herd of white-tailed deer
in our legs, the bobcat across our shoulders,
and from our hearts, the indigo bunting
powering its fast blue open to take in
the dancer with the dance.

August 7, 2011: Tuttle Creek Lake, Kansas (above & right). Elevated thunderstorm/updraft base on stationary front. The Holy Grail in storm photography is the combination of stars and lightning. The scene requires both clear skies and storm clouds. My position, south of a stationary front, enabled me to obtain these conditions for several hours.

Whoever You Are, Come Back

This is what the waters always tell us:
rolling away from and toward us in the dark,
reminding us of everything that formed us
in the darkness before our cells even clustered
enough toward some kind of knowing.
The shine in the sky, on the lake, speaks light to light
in a language of rain, longing, explosions above,
depth below, and horizons beyond too far to comprehend.

This storm lands, face to face, in the center of this lake:
this dream we return to, recognizing the lapis moment
that the stars burn through the thinning clouds.
Whoever is lost is found here. Whatever lines old loves
followed or lost sight of no longer bind us apart.
Let us hear this wind, feel it sweep our faces clean,
surrender to whoever we are and aren't. Let us return.

August 17, 2009: Watonga, Oklahoma. Supercell, anvil lightning bolt. An Anvil bolt, originates in the highest regions of a cumulonimbus cloud. Such bolts can occur some distance away from the parent thunderstorm updraft and often strike in an open area ahead of the storm. Sometimes they leave a smoking crater in the ground. I made this image from the relative safety of my vehicle, not standing outside because the storm had a history of producing such lightning.

August 17, 2009: Watonga, OK. Supercell, cloud-to-ground lighting. An old outflow boundary from early morning convection provided the focus for this isolated supercell. Because the jet stream flow was relatively light, this storm did not move for over an hour. Fueled by high August instability, it sustained a persistent updraft. I shot the entire storm from a single vantage point.

Light

for Stan

Every act an exchange of light with light,
Stan says as we sit on lawn chairs in the sun.
Gravity catches everything: the falling down,
the fear of harm, the harm anyway along lines
thought tapless, nonexistent, all made from
flecks of light, even our comfortable bones
magnet to magnet to the sun, the moon,
whatever catches the light.

Everything we see travels this way—
the shimmering starling landing on the roof,
the first pin oak leaf detaching, the pebbles
under our feet, the squirrel gathering its winter all fall.
Light makes one live moment out of a dead one
as we sit under the sun, miniaturized from
the eight minutes it takes to land here.

When I fall asleep, when I fall in love,
when I trip in the hall and catch myself
it's all gravity, which loves us all so much
it can't help but to pull us close, show us
the floor, and then how to draw on the light
to push ourselves back up.

August 19, 2009: Sedan, Kansas. Convection and cloud-to-ground lightning in the flanking line south of a tornadic supercell. After busting in Oklahoma with no severe storms, I was feeling dejected. Luckily, while driving home to Kansas City, I managed to intercept this storm on Highway 166 west of Sedan, Kansas. This has become a favorite image, and I feel it redeems the unsuccessful trip to Oklahoma.

Interlude

First, the square of sky opens its wide door
while lightning or headlights ignite the future.

Then the colors band together like animals
of different herds before fading to black.

The distant flash says, *something happened,*
is happening still at the intersections of dark and light

The shield of sky dissolves, the animals underground
or sheltered in the eaves of trees, tentatively pour back out.

The bats funnel from one set of trees into another.
Life threads itself through time's needle.

In the morning, all returns, dim at its edges and dewy
as if the world is starting over again, which it is.

Climate Is What You Expect, Weather Is What You Get

But that doesn't stop us from yearning
for warmth and long life in the spacious house
of climate, seemingly safe from weather
even if weather built this house. Our bodies
crave solid ground when the actual earth
is fluid as sky, just slower, changing in the dinging
of small hail. Heat evaporates from the sidewalk
on the eastern edge of the cold front, making itself up
as it goes along, just like the space between skyscrapers
invents its own weather. Streets everywhere reflect
the city's hunger and ingenuity in the headlights,
stars speeding toward us, of all the weather we are.

August 20, 2010: Kansas City, Missouri. Cloud to ground lightning. This photograph is the view from a vantage point at historic Strawberry Hill in Kansas City, Kansas, looking east. Because storms typically travel east, I sometimes visit this location to photograph the backside of storms as they leave the city. During this mid-summer chase, I occupied one of my favorite perches in front of the Croatian church with a clear view of the city across the river.

September 13, 2010: Westmoreland, Kansas. Cloud-to-ground lightning. Good photography can require a bit of luck, and one can take steps to improve the odds. With that in mind, I recognized a recurring pattern of lightning in the direction I wanted. Then I was able to predict this shot through the pasture gate.

Your Heart Has No Gate

No fenceposts to hang a gate from either,
nothing even to enclose. How can you hold the wind
when it sweeps through the stubble field of your sorrow?
What belongs here as opposed to there?

Don't you see, little sister, old father,
boy on the brink of man, small child,
that there never was, never could be an actual way
to hold back, not from this sweet motor of synapse
and fire that turns you toward the moment arriving
in each breath. Don't you already know that
your life is a flock of birds filling every branch
on the windswept cedar?

The scraps of lumber you place here, or how
you stay far back from the borderland
does not make an actual gate. A comfort maybe
but no gate. The vigorous gymnastics
of your thoughts lift and propel you, but still,
the heart trembles in its nest; takes in, releases
all your blood every four minutes;
releases itself into the stippled blues and greens
of the awakening world. It knows no other truth
than what it makes when you acknowledge
there's nothing to protect, but everything to save.

Flight Plan

My heart trills its plans, a cardinal on a rusting swing set.
It fears how fast the grass grows but knows life also resists mowing or fire.

In winter, it bursts red from cedars through snow fog.
In summer, it sounds an alarm in the dense green roar of cicadas.

My heart twists itself in longing to sing its mechanics into enchantment.
It meteors across the sky and lands on a dime.

Perched in the dark, alert day or night, mated or lonely, old or young, it never
leaves the nest of this body, yet travels like weather in its trembling imagination.

When it storms, my heart drops into a single streak of lightning
from ocean above to the ocean below.

September 18, 2010: Perry Lake, Kansas. Tornadic supercell, cloud-to-ground lightning. This storm was a prolific cloud-to-ground lightning generator, so I did not dare leave my vehicle. I shot this with a window-mounted camera. This lightning bolt occurred in the precise location within the frame to make a nice composition. So often in chasing, conditions fail—storms don't cooperate, camera angles don't work out, but every once in a while, you get a perfect shot.

September 19, 2013: Kansas City, Missouri. Shelf cloud. A shelf cloud entered Kansas City and defined a line of thunderstorms producing cloud-to-ground lightning and heavy rain. Shortly after making this image, I hurriedly took refuge in the Liberty Memorial World War I Museum where, soaking wet, I inadvertently interrupted a cocktail party.

Memorial

Behind this building, another. Inside, windows within windows.
Outside, the skyline lined with sky. The arches within and beyond:
made of night. The highway: from daylight and men who knew
this hill long before there were losses to memorialize. The trees
wait, patiently shuffling the wind. The flag snaps, then pours out
its length of memory. The ghost army of storm clouds march east,
the streets charcoal in the shine of rain that makes people steer
with their shoulders. The slim breezes of love the dead left behind
a century ago cycle through this weather, a downpour so hard
that neither the dead nor the living can hear themselves think,
and even the fountains can't say if they're rising or falling.

Two Bodies Always in Motion

A coruscating kaleidescope of fire, grief,
possibility, and beauty about to be ghosted
in the velvet memory of stars and eyes.

One body bends its light toward land,
the other mirrors its mirage into tall sky.
Yellow-bellied heavens ring jewel tones
of flicker, low notes of boom.

Skirts of electrical impulse rustle
stage curtains across the Great Plains.
What we call a sunbow, neon way of knowing,
thumbprint of the sun, lost ship of florescence
tipping its arctic ridges south
before vanishing north for another decade.

The light never leaves us, only wavers.
No one ever lost completely except
in one slot of time, one way of loving.
Always two bodies: our own, and the world's.

October 24, 2011: Perry Lake, Kansas. Aurora. On Monday October 24, 2011 at approximately 1:00 PM Earth was struck by a coronal mass ejection. The impact strongly compressed Earth's magnetic field and sparked an intense geomagnetic storm. As night fell over North America auroras spilled across the Canadian border into the contiguous United States. In a rare reverberation the storm pushed south to Kansas. My cameras were ready.

October 14, 2013: West of Claflin, Kansas. Thunderstorm at sunset. This barn west of Claflin, Kansas, silently struggles to bear its own weight beneath the storm and witness yet another Kansas sunset.

Possession

Have the sun right there in the west on its own time,
ready to fall away exactly when it should.

Have the cello late at night between your legs, your right arm aching
as you try to press one note into another.

Have the waltz in your mind. Have the orange in the large gray bowl,
your fingers holding its scent of new light and promise.

Have the walls clean for a day after painting before the kids come
with their expressive hands. Have yourself stretching low, washcloth in hand.

Have the paper, blank and abundant, the easy glow of black blue
at night, the morning fog lifting as if it's never been there.

Have the dream of short palm trees hiding the machinery of cancer
while men embrace in T'ai Chi and heal each other before your very eyes.

Have a mother and her small daughter hopping on one foot in front
of the Victorian house in disrepair. Have the squirrels watch.

Have the voice speaking almost Yiddish in your mind,
the siren of coyotes, and the double whistle of trains you can't see.

Have recognition and wonder, turquoise earrings, a car that starts
in winter, one thick wool sweater under your coat.

Have love too—all you're willing to join with,
plentiful as air. And the peace of not wanting.

Balancing on the Equinox

The golden tree holds her pose
for several breaths in a dazzle
of wind, rise, feather and run.
Meantime, time falls from the trees.
A man on a bicycle pumps hard up the hill.
A black lab tears down the street,
leash flying behind him.
One white plastic bag pauses
at the side of the tree: a flag or spirit
before dropping down to trash again.

I stand in the backyard in tree:
my right leg trembling as it supports me,
my left knee bent, leading the hip open.
I press my palms together at my heart
and wish for balance while falling.
The storm to come cups the west side
of this life. The heat of summer cups the right.
The golden tree holds very still, then surrenders
everything to the wide arms of the world.

October 30, 2013: Northeast Kansas fog. Forecasting fog is one of the exasperating aspects of my job. In my area of northeast Kansas, it is difficult and unusual to foretell the required conditions. I spend a lot of time pouring over temperature, dew point, wind, and sky cover data to predict what will happen overnight. Moreover, microclimates play a role. Such was the case this morning when southerly breezes were warming the atmosphere, causing fog to dissipate in most areas except on the north side of hills where this image was made.

November 25, 2013: Wyandotte County Lake, Kansas. Morning fog. On this particular day the fog forecast was marginal, but this lake, close to a river valley, often produces a fog when most areas won't. While driving, there was no fog until I arrived at water's edge.

Love Dissolves Your Name

When love comes, the contours
of the shoreline dissolve:
no longer you against the odds,
or your worth pulled in
by the undercurrent
you thought birthed you.
The false bottom drops out.
The lake clears. What lives
filters through walnut leaves,
stills to show the naked light
framing everything. You
inhale your arms overhead,
a gesture of flight and height,
your heart vulnerable but open,
your fingers spread to reach,
the chevron in your back
articulating itself. Overhead,
a flock of red-winged blackbirds,
flashing fire, and behind you,
the silhouetted husks
of sunflowers, long burnt
to silence by the cold.
You exhale through the fog
toward the sun. A blue heron
lands on the other side.
Without missing a beat,
you step into the water.
The cold clarity of morning
restores you, just like love.

Still Life

No sun. No wind. Only the bevelled surface
of land and lake. Time looks at his hand,
amazed how the lines have deepened,
how years have quieted the thrashing heart.
Nothing needs to fall into place or apart.
The red branches spell out the next perch
to land on, weigh into wind, lift off from
to the mirror of the lake. The mirror of the sky
holds the redbuds of the season ahead
and behind, the seeds of all those blossoms
quiverless in the trembling breath of winter.
No reason to cross over, no reason not to.
Stand in the center of the bridge. Consider
the still lives of fruit and flower, snow and birch,
you and the migrating constellations
configuring this breath, and the next one.

December 26, 2009: Kansas City, Missouri. Loose Park foot-bridge, snowstorm. I trudged through very wet heavy snow with my tripod to make this image. Additionally, snow was actually melting when it hit my camera, making it very wet, so I had to shield the lens. This is what I call an urban snow chase.

February 1, 2011: Kansas City, Missouri. Country Club Plaza, urban blizzard. The point here was to play the intense fuchsia-colored lanterns against the cold snow, but it was snowing so hard I struggled to keep the snow off the lens. I had these lanterns in the back of my mind for months and anticipated I would use them in a photo when conditions were favorable. On this day, conditions were just what I had hoped for.

When February Comes

We won't forget what the sky can do:
everything erased by the snow, layering
the spaces between railing and hand.
We won't be bound by time, only shovels,
heat and the wonders of what can be made
with few ingredients. We won't be confined
by sinewy memory or curvaceous plans
that lead us beyond the terrain of our quietest
stories. Instead, we will land squarely on this day
in the center of the blizzard that mixes sky and land,
wind and verticality, slants of climbing snow.
We will stand at the window before the hard waves
of winter, the dizzy of a billion snowflakes,
the stern-hearted cedar shaking its head,
the one red bird balancing on a slim branch,
everything and everyone watching the earth dream.

No Other Way

The river sings through rock and time as we sit at its bank.
Our truest wishes rise from underground tributaries composed
of old ocean, lost beloveds, bravest bones, clearest seeing.

What we know winters over into porous ground.
What we don't know lands on high branches only the deer see.

We turn our faces faithfully toward moonlight and motion,
waiting for what comes next. A bluebird returns to the harmonics
of cedar and big bluestem. The night and temperature fall.

We remember that this world holds and holds us together
in the widening river of stars, above as below. No other way.

March 28, 2009: East of Greensburg, Kansas. Tunnel cut through snowdrift by locomotive. This snowdrift is notable because it's a spring blizzard that set a Kansas state record for snowfall at the rate of 30 inches in 24 hours. That wall on the right side is about 10 feet high. Locomotives plowed through the snowdrift forming a canyon.

March 28, 2009: East of Pratt, Kansas. Spring blizzard snowdrifts. The snowdrifts are in front of red cedars (a form of juniper) making this scene look more like Colorado than Kansas.

March 28, 2009. East of Greensburg, Kansas. Thistle seed head in the snowdrifts from a spring blizzard. I was drawn to the austerity of this photo: the wind-blown tundra-like landscape with a lone thistle popping out. I had a sense of the way life goes dormant and hangs on through the cold winter.